365 DAYS OF YOGA

Sarah Richardson

summersdale

365 DAYS OF YOGA

Copyright © Summersdale Publishers Ltd, 2015

Text compiled by Sarah Richardson

All rights reserved.

Sarah Richardson has asserted her right to be identified as the author of this work in accordance with sections 77 and 78 of the Copyright, Designs and Patents Act 1988.

Summersdale Publishers Ltd
46 West Street
Chichester
West Sussex
PO19 1RP
UK

www.summersdale.com

Printed and bound in the Czech Republic

ISBN: 978-1-84953-666-0

To...

From...

Introduction

At the centre of yoga is you. Yoga helps you to build harmony between your body, mind and spirit to create a calmer, stronger, healthier and happier you.

If you are a beginner, pace yourself and take things slowly. Yoga is not a competition. It does not matter who can get themselves tied into the tightest knot, or who can hold a position the longest; it is about finding your equilibrium and pace. Nothing is rushed, movement is slow, breathing is long and deep and relaxation is integral to your practice.

Observe your body at all times and respond to how you feel. Strength and stamina build over time, so move away from discomfort or pain in your muscles. Repeat a stretch as many times as you feel is right for you and always do the same stretch to both sides of your body to keep it balanced. Keep comfortable; remember, yoga is joyful practice.

Yoga is best practised on a non-slip yoga mat and with bare feet. If you have any concerns with regards your health, or if you are pregnant, always seek advice from a medical professional or qualified yoga teacher.

This book is a springboard into the year ahead, full of daily inspirations, healthy living tips, suggested yoga poses and stretches to help you take each day at a time. This is a gift for you.

JANUARY

1 Remember, you are your own teacher. Listen carefully to how your body feels and refrain from straining. Rather than forcing your body, breathe and relax into a position. Move away from pain and discomfort during any stretch and take things slowly.

2 Whenever you find yourself standing still, practise Mountain. Inhale: engage your legs and thighs, stabilise your core, lift through your chest. Exhale: roll your shoulders back and pull them down the spine.

The most important pieces of equipment you need for doing yoga are your body and your mind.

Rodney Yee

 Before and after your practice, relax in Corpse to still the body. Lie on your back, feet relaxed and apart, arms away from your body, palms facing up. Focus on your breath to still your mind.

Replace tea and coffee with herbal tea or hot water to help flush toxins from your body. Start the year afresh!

 Yoga breathing involves inhalation and exhalation through your nose. The tiny hairs in your nasal passage naturally filter the air before it enters your lungs. Bring this awareness into everyday breathing to inhale clean air into your body.

 The symbol *om* represents what is understood to be the vibrational sound of the universe.

Start writing a diary dedicated to your yoga practice. This safe place is where you can reflect on your thoughts, feelings and observations in order to develop honest communication with yourself.

 In yoga, a posture or position is called an *asana*. Synchronised with your breathing, an *asana* is entered, held and exited with control. Practise your favourite *asana*, slowing breath and movement to gain optimum control.

10 Ease tension from your facial muscles at any time in Lion. Inhale: tightly scrunch your face. Exhale through your mouth with a 'roar'. Drop your jaw, open your eyes wide and extend your tongue.

 11 Strengthen your arms and shoulders in Plank. Lie on your front, ensuring your wrists are below your shoulders. Lift your body off the mat, and hold and breathe in position. Pull the heels of your feet together. Build your stamina by holding the pose a little longer each day.

12 Release emotional energy stored in your hips by practising Bridge. Lie on your back. Inhale. Exhale: bend your knees and place your feet on the floor. Inhale: push your hips into the air. Hold and breathe for as long as you feel comfortable.

Yoga is the perfect opportunity to be curious about who you are.

Jason Crandell

14 Breathe in Lunge to encourage muscle relief in your groin and thighs. Start on  all fours. Inhale: bring your left foot between your hands, with toes and fingertips in line. Exhale: sink into the back of your right thigh. Repeat on the other side.

 15 A *mudra* is a hand gesture that seals or locks your energy; yoga for your hands. Bring the tips of the thumb and index finger together on  both hands and extend the remaining fingers in *Gyan Mudra* to promote clarity of mind during meditation.

Observe Three-Part Breathing to empower your everyday breathing pattern. During inhalation feel your stomach rise, then your ribcage expand, and finally your chest inflate. As you exhale feel your chest fall, followed by your ribs, and then your stomach.

 Rest your liver; have an alcohol-free week. Monitor any physical or emotional reactions you experience in your diary. You may choose to modify your drinking habits for longer.

Breathing is one of the greatest secrets of yoga – if you practise, it will obtain emotional powers beyond your imagination.

Bija Bennett

 Yoga works on relieving the body in many ways, including releasing wind. There is no need to feel embarrassed, instead feel happy that yoga is doing its job!

Use a mantra (*man* meaning mind, *tra* meaning instrument), a sound vibration that is repeated aloud or in your head, to connect mind with spirit during meditation. *Om* (pronounced 'a-au-m') is a popular mantra.

 Keep your eyes closed throughout your practice to deepen your concentration on your internal world. 'See' your body from the inside out.

 You can use a folded blanket to sit on or to place under your knees to make yourself comfortable during your practice. Cover yourself with it during relaxation to retain your body heat.

23 Breathe in Child to ease discomfort in your lower back. Start on all fours. Inhale: stretch your tail bone skywards. Exhale: slowly lower your buttocks to your heels, forehead to the earth. Bring your arms by your side, with your fingers in line with your toes.

24 Scan your body for aches, pains, stresses and tension in Corpse before your practice to tune into how your body feels in the present moment.

Bring your hands together, leaving a little hollow space between your palms, in peaceful Prayer, *Atmanjali Mudra*, to harmonise left and right brain hemispheres. This *mudra* calms thoughts and creates harmony, peace and balance within oneself.

Practice makes the heart grow fonder.

Stephanie Pappas

27

You can't do anything about the length of your life, but you can do something about its width and depth.

Shira Tehrani

28 Cross-legged, or Happy Seat, is the most popular position for meditation. Place cushions under your knees to make yourself comfortable, allowing your hips to open without strain.

Tune into your feelings to stay connected with your emotional self. Ask, 'How do I feel right here, right now?' Listen to your answer and react appropriately.

 Your feet carry you everywhere you go. Treat them to a warm foot soak at the end of a long day to show them your loving gratitude.

 Follow a sequence of forward or backward bends with a twist to neutralise your spine and to release any pressure. Inhale: raise your hands above your head. Exhale: lower your left hand across the front of your body and your right hand behind you. Feel the twist in your waist and through your torso. Repeat on the opposite side.

FEBRUARY

1 Watch something funny or laugh out loud just for the sake of it! When you laugh endorphins are released, your mood is lightened and your stomach muscles get a gentle workout.

2 Squeeze your shoulder blades together to energise the area. Inhale: raise your arms above your head. Exhale: lower them behind your back, interlock your fingers and extend your arms. Inhale: bring the heels of your hands together. Exhale: release.

In yoga, breath control is called *pranayama* (*prana* meaning universal energy, *yama* meaning control). Optimising and controlling your daily breathing patterns will help reduce stress levels and maintain a healthy body and mind.

 On World Meditation days, which occur on the first Sunday of every month, do a simple sensory meditation. Take a few minutes to notice what you can see, hear, smell, taste and feel. Whenever you slip back into thinking, gently bring your focus back to your senses.

5 In any position requiring balance, focus on a fixed point in front of you to enhance your concentration and stabilise your position. This is known as the *dristi* point.

6 Feel steady and strong in Warrior I. Start in Lunge. Inhale: straighten and extend your right leg back. Exhale: squeeze into your buttocks to stabilise your lower back. 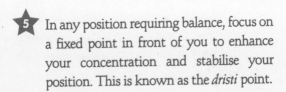 Inhale: bring your hands above your head. Repeat, stretching out your left leg.

When you're planning your next vacation, consider choosing an activity holiday that combines a holiday with an interest. Horse riding? Sailing? Pottery? Cycling? Whatever you choose, it'll be right for you.

 Muscle has memory. If your practice has lapsed, do not be deterred. Get back onto your mat, and your muscles will be happy to gently ease back into familiar stretches.

 Uplift your spirits by playing your favourite dance tunes. Turn up the volume and dance like no one cares, not even you!

10

There's no half-singing in the shower, you're either a rock star or an opera diva.

Josh Groban

11 Love your body, learn to accept and be happy with how you look. Move away from judging, and celebrate how amazing you and your body truly are.

12

Be a lamp to yourself.
Be your own confidence.
Hold on to the truth within
yourself as to the only truth.

Buddha

 Instead of reaching for the headache
tablets, kick off your shoes and rub
your big toes, which represent your
head in reflexology. Massage them to
send healing energy to your headache.
Remember to drink water as headaches
can be a result of dehydration.

14 Breathe away February blues through a breathing meditation. Inhale for the count of eight, exhale for the count of 16. Deeper relaxation is achieved through deeper exhalation.

 15 Move in Clock to open your shoulders. Stand with your left shoulder and hip in contact with a wall. Inhale: raise your left arm against the wall to a 12 o'clock position. Exhale: lower it to one o'clock. Continue moving around the clock, breathing alternately in and out on each 'hour'. Repeat on right side.

16 Throughout the day, rotate your ankles one way, then the other to keep your joints warm, flexible and mobile when the weather is cold.

 17 Notice how the daylight hours are getting longer in the evening and enjoy the thought that spring is around the corner.

 18 Shake, shake, shake to free yourself of an unwanted feeling or negative vibration. Relax your muscles, loosen your joints and shake. Visualise any negative feelings evaporating.

19 Sit in Staff to lengthen your hamstrings and to improve your posture. Sit with both legs extended. Inhale: use your hands to pull the flesh of your buttocks away from your tail bone to connect your 'sit bones' to your mat. Exhale: lengthen your spine and place your palms to the earth.

20 Eat slowly to aid digestion. Put your knife and fork down and take breaks between mouthfuls, allowing time for your taste buds to savour the array of flavours in your food.

21 Stroke your face from jaw line to cheeks using your fingertips and light, rapid upward movements. This will stimulate blood flow, creating a warm glow and an instant facelift!

22

The quickest way to experiencing the peace inside is to learn to recognise when I am not at peace.

Jim McDonald

Crying is like laughing; it helps to free and cleanse the soul. Give yourself permission to release your tears and let them flow.

Sow love, reap peace. Sow meditation, reap wisdom.

Swami Sivānanda Saraswati

25 Strengthen the soles of your feet to improve standing balances. Inhale: slowly rise onto the balls of your feet. Exhale: lower your heels slowly to the earth. Inhale: rock back onto your heels, lift your toes. Exhale: lower your toes. Repeat at least three times.

 26 Listen to your body. If you are recovering from an injury, refrain from participating in a full practice to allow sufficient time for your body to heal.

Clean your feet daily, especially before you stand on your yoga mat, to help keep your mat fresh.

 Can you live a day without spending any money? Challenge yourself to try.

 This day only appears once every four years. View it as an opportunity to do something special for yourself and make the most of the additional day!

MARCH

⭐ **1** Brighten up a space in your home. Decorate the paintwork and walls to freshen it up. Enjoy the process of planning, preparation and productivity and the added satisfaction of energy well spent.

 2 Bring yoga breathing into your everyday movements to allow your body to function to its maximum potential. Before you bend to pick something up, inhale. Bend on your exhalation, and then inhale as you straighten up.

What did you enjoy doing as a child? Flying a kite? Feeding the ducks? Playing a musical instrument? Go ahead – rekindle a childhood delight. Do it today!

 Take a mindful moment to prepare your body for action if you have been sitting for a long time and your muscles have been inactive. Before you move, think, 'I am ready,' and inhale as you stand. Fill your lungs with new energy to prepare yourself to move.

Floss daily to reduce plaque and if you have not been to the dentist recently, make an appointment so your smile will sparkle at its best.

 Seize the opportunity of a nice day to take your practice outside and breathe in the freshness of the spring air.

 Listen carefully to how you speak to nurture a positive approach in your thinking. Change your expression from 'I can't' to 'I can' and reap the positive rewards.

Declutter your physical space to make space in your life, physically and mentally. Target an overloaded wardrobe, the packed-to-within-an-inch-of-its-life garden shed or an overflowing kitchen drawer.

 Spring is in the air! Open windows and doors to remove stale energy. Allow the fresh spring breeze to flow through your house and refresh your space.

For a day or two after your practice, regardless of your fitness level, you may feel gentle aches in your muscles where they have been working hard. Feel encouraged. These sensations will pass and they actually show that your muscles are getting stronger!

 Now is the moment of power. Change procrastination into positive action and feel your emotional energy lighten as a result.

When the breath wanders, the mind is unsteady, but when the breath is still, so is the mind still.

Yoga Pradipika

 Rub your scalp with small circular movements, as if you are washing your hair, to stimulate nerve endings under your scalp and to help soothe tension.

Give yourself a break.
When you are alone
with your thoughts, you
shouldn't be arguing.

Gary Rudz

 Remind yourself during the day to roll your shoulders back and pull your shoulder blades down your spine to encourage good posture. Keep your chest lifted to boost a feeling of confidence.

16 Gently flex your spine in Cow. Start on all fours. Inhale: tip your tail bone skyward, dip your navel towards the floor, lift your head. Exhale: tilt your head back, look skywards.

17 Work with a yoga block to provide support as you build on your flexibility and deepen your practice.

18 Send focused healing energy to an area of discomfort in the body with *Mukula Mudra*. Bring the tips of your fingers and thumb of one hand together, like a bird's beak, and place on the area of unease. Connect and breathe for several minutes.

Massage your lower back in Happy Baby. Lie on your back. Inhale: bring your knees to your chest, direct the soles of your feet skywards. Grab your feet with your hands, allowing your knees to relax and fall out to the sides. Exhale: gently rock side to side.

 Spring-clean your yoga mat with a spritz of water mixed with a few drops of tea tree essence oil, which has natural disinfectant qualities.

Yin and yang reflect the two opposites in nature: moon/sun, female/male, cold/hot, dark/bright. The yin/yang symbol represents how together they balance, reflect and harmonise each other to create a whole.

 Take a trip to the countryside or a walk through the park or woods to revel in the signs of spring as nature wakens from hibernation. Breathe in the energy!

Build stamina in your abdominal muscles with Leg Raises. Lie on your back, arms by your sides, palms down. Inhale: lift your leg, directing the sole of your foot towards the sky. Hold for three breaths, lower as you exhale. Raise your legs individually or together.

 Set a calming mood to create a soothing environment for your practice. Perhaps burn incense or a scented aromatherapy candle, dim the lighting, play gentle meditation music or have a natural object nearby.

25

Wheresoever you go, go with all your heart.

Confucius

26 After spending time in Corpse, wriggle your fingers and toes, and flex and stretch your feet to wake your body slowly. Inhale: stretch your hands over your head. Exhale: relax your arms back to your sides.

27 Choose today to try a meat-free diet for the next three days, week or however long suits you. Get your protein through eggs, nuts, cheese or beans. Note any differences in how you feel in your yoga diary.

In the midst of movement and chaos, keep stillness inside of you.

Deepak Chopra

29 Notice the difference in evening light as the clocks go forward by an hour for summer time!

 30 Improve circulation while also strengthening your calves. Walk up an escalator instead of standing, or use stairs instead of the lift. Keep active and strong and get your heart muscle pumping!

 31 Set yourself a new goal to challenge your mind and body. Work towards achieving a new *asana*.

APRIL

1 Look out for rainbows in the sky during April showers to remind you of the wonders of nature. Let the colourful light fill you with happiness.

2 Nurture a plant. Water it regularly, keep it in sunlight, and watch it grow daily... just like you.

3 Explore the meaning of yoga – unity. From Happy Seat, bring the soles of your feet together. Wrap your hands around them and focus on the point of union between left and right.

Shop at local businesses or markets to support your local traders.

 Be your best friend, not your enemy. Smile in the mirror and tell yourself, 'I love you.'

 After each *asana,* or flow, you practise, breathe deeply until your heartbeat is stabilised to allow the blood flow to become steady.

The muscles in your body are interconnected. They twist, turn, contract, lengthen, tense and relax. Visualise your muscles softening and loosening during relaxation to let go of tension.

 Swing your arms to shift blocked energy. Stand in Mountain. Inhale and exhale as you swing your arms forwards and backwards. Clap your hands whenever they come together.

9

Remember the emphasis on the heart. The mind lives in doubt and the heart lives in trust. When you trust, suddenly you become centred.

Osho

10 Switch off your TV, give yourself a break from Facebook and Twitter and spend a night in with a yoga book from the library. Research your favourite *asana*.

If you change the way you look at things, the things you look at change.

Wayne Dyer

 Remove stale air to make way for oxygen-rich air with *Kapalbhati* breathing. Inhale a long, silent breath and allow your stomach to swell. Exhale: contract your stomach muscles sharply with a brief audible breath. Repeat several times, breathing in and out through your nose.

Place your hands, one on top of the other with your palms facing up, and your thumbs touching in *Dhyana Mudra*. This hand gesture means meditation, and provides completeness during meditative moments.

 Invigorate your energy flow in Seated Forward Bend. Begin in Staff. Inhale: raise your hands above your head. Exhale: unhinge from the hips and fold forward keeping your spine straight. Hold your shins, ankles or toes depending on your flexibility and breathe for as long as you feel comfortable.

Create some time for yourself. Book a day off work and indulge in a 'free to be me day' and do whatever you feel like doing.

 Try a simple breathing technique to help still and quieten the mind. Inhale for the count of six, exhale for the count of 12. Come back to your breath if your mind wanders.

 Be present in every moment today. Remember you have choice in everything you do.

Lie on your back with your buttocks against a wall and your legs vertically up the wall to revive tired legs. Inhale: stretch your legs upwards. Exhale: rest your arms out to the sides, palms up. Breathe deeply and hold for as long as you feel comfortable.

 Take a walking meditation to clear your mind. Centre yourself. Focus on the 'lightness' as you lift each foot, the 'motion' as each foot extends forwards, and the 'heaviness' as you place each foot on the ground.

20 When you are lying on your back, uncurl and straighten your tail bone to lengthen your spine.

 21 When your hands and feet come into contact with your mat, mindfully create a firm connection to stabilise yourself. This is called *bandha*, meaning lock. *Hasta bandha* means hand lock, and *Pada bandha* means foot lock.

 22 To trim your waist and strengthen your core, inhale and circle your hands above your head. As you exhale, lower your left arm by your side and gently lean to the left. Repeat on the opposite side.

Have fun in Upturned Beetle to loosen the muscles around your joints. Lie on your back. Inhale and lift your arms and legs into the air and shake. Keep your muscles floppy and relaxed.

A truly flexible back makes for a long life.

Chinese proverb

Make a detailed and specific list of 30 things you want for yourself in your life. When an entry is fulfilled, cross it from your list. Add something else to keep your list topped up to 30. Celebrate each achievement and give thanks for the gifts in your life.

 Actively say 'thank you' to show your appreciation to others.

 Tap into your creative self – paint a canvas, decorate a cake, make a pom-pom or whatever tickles your fancy. Allow yourself to play and be creative.

28 Observe spring bulbs, such as tulips and daffodils, as they shoot up from the dark. Think about the abundance of energy and natural information that lets each bulb know it's springtime!

 29 Hold and breathe in a Squat to open up your groin and release compression to the lower back. Start in Mountain. Inhale: lift onto your toes. Exhale: bend your knees and slowly lower buttocks to heels.

 30 Give a powerful stretch to the whole body in Downward Dog. Start in Plank. Inhale. As you exhale, lift your tail bone skywards, push back with your hands and bring your heels to the earth.

Connect with your inner spirit in Warrior II. Start in Mountain. Inhale: step back with your left foot. Exhale: bend your right knee. Inhale. Exhale: extend your right arm forwards, your left arm behind. Hold for as long as you feel strong. Repeat on the other side.

 Indulge and have fun; go on a yoga retreat for the long weekend.

The palms of the hands are powerful sensors of energy. To increase energy flow at any time: inhale, and as you exhale, spread your fingers wide apart and stretch across your palms. Hold for three breaths. Relax your hands on an exhalation.

 Life is challenging, full of surprises and change is inevitable. Yoga can help you embrace life's challenges positively with calmness and flexibility.

 Roast sesame seeds to give them a nutty taste and to add a rich assortment of minerals to your food. Heat in a hot, dry frying pan until they turn golden brown, then sprinkle onto salads and fruit.

Chakras are non-physical energy points in the body. Seven of the most important *chakras* lie along the spine, from your 'root' (genital area) to the crown of your head. Each *chakra* is associated with a different colour.

 After any inversion, when your head has been below your heart (as in Standing Forward Bend, Child and Shoulder Stand), close your eyes as you straighten to avoid a light-headed feeling or dizziness.

Relax in Lizard to allow rest time during your practice. Lie on your front. Inhale: make a cushion for your head with your hands. Exhale: bend your left knee out to the side, keeping it connect to the ground. This help to open your hip. Repeat on the other side.

 Include a Crescent Lunge in your practice to acknowledge the crescent moon appearing in the sky. Start in Lunge. Inhale: tighten your buttocks for stability, bring your hands above your head, palms facing each other. Release the position on your exhalation.

Before you go to sleep, reflect on your day. Look for the positive in all your experiences and give thanks.

 Write a letter or send a card through the post to say hello to someone who is dear to you.

 Fold into Standing Forward Bend to allow blood flow to revitalise your brain. Start in Mountain. Inhale. Exhale as you fold forwards from your hips, aiming to connect your palms with the earth. Bend your knees slightly if they feel tight.

Let food be thy medicine and medicine be thy food.

Hippocrates

 If your stomach feels uncomfortable, incorporate some extra twists into your practice to detox and boost your digestive system.

Remember, it doesn't matter how deep into a posture you go – what does matter is who you are when you get there.

Max Strom

 Do your practice in controlled, super slow motion today to draw your attention to how your body feels.

Lie still in this gentle hip-opening meditation to bring relaxation to the ligaments around your hips. Lie on your back, join the soles of your feet together. Breathe and relax into the position. Hold for as long as you feel comfortable.

 Draw imaginary circles with your hip, knee and ankle joints to keep them flexible and loose. Balance on one foot freeing the opposite leg to explore small and large circular movements in each joint.

19 Rub your hands together and gently place your palms over your eyes to create a dark place to soothe tired and irritated eyes from a day of high pollen count. Breathe.

 20 Balance in Warrior III to improve circulation. Start in Mountain. Inhale: slowly lift your left leg behind you. Exhale: lower your torso parallel to the earth. Stretch your arms forwards. Breathe and hold still for as long as you feel comfortable. Repeat on the right side.

Before you move into a twist, focus on lengthening your spine and lifting your chest upwards as you inhale. The additional lift in your torso will yield a deeper twist.

 Make a list of your good habits and the not-so-good ones in your yoga diary. Be honest. Look at changing any behaviour that does not serve you.

 Dedicate some time to learning about your anatomy. Familiarise yourself with the name and function of your muscles. Study their shape and size and where they attach to deepen your level of understanding.

24 Make a light snoring sound at the back of your throat as the air enters your body, in *Ujjayi*, or Ocean Breath. Tap into *Ujjayi* breathing to empower your inhalation and tone your epiglottis, which lies at the base of your tongue.

 25 Be graceful in Dancer. Begin in Mountain. Inhale: raise your left foot behind you. Exhale: hold your foot with your left hand. Inhale: raise your right hand above your head. Exhale: slowly lower your torso forward. Inhale and release the position as you exhale. Repeat on the opposite side.

To increase the energy flow in your spine, practise Cat. Start on all fours. Inhale. Exhale: curl your tail bone, arch your back and look towards your navel. Breathe. Hold and then release. Repeat as many times as you enjoy.

27

When you find peace within yourself, you become the kind of person who can live at peace with others.

Peace Pilgrim

We can learn a lot from each other: share your knowledge.

Be at least as interested in what goes on inside you as what happens outside. If you get the inside right, the outside will fall into place.

Eckhart Tolle

Life would be a dull place if we were all the same. Live and let live. Avoid comparing yourself to others, celebrate the differences and be happy to be you.

 Aloha is a Hawaiian greeting and also means 'to love and be happy with'. Bring the Hawaiian spirit of aloha into your day.

JUNE

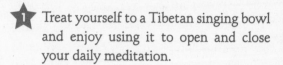

1 Treat yourself to a Tibetan singing bowl and enjoy using it to open and close your daily meditation.

2 Enjoy a selfless act, known as *karma* yoga. Donate some of your time and energy today to someone who needs your help, company or support.

3 Blow on a fully seeded dandelion head and watch the seeds drift away to make a new life elsewhere.

Reflect and observe any changes you have experienced during your yoga journey so far. Perhaps your general energy levels have increased, maybe you are feeling stronger, calmer, more flexible? Yoga has many benefits, how has it benefitted you?

 Breathe to centre yourself in Thunderbolt. Kneel with your buttocks resting on the soles of your feet. Rest your palms on your knees and lengthen through your spine. This is a comfortable seated position for meditation.

6 Visit a lake, fountain, waterfall, river or the sea to experience the relaxing pleasure of all of your senses responding to the nearness of water.

 7 Lift into Inclined Plank to invigorate your heart. Start in Staff. Put your hands on the ground behind you, fingertips pointing away. Inhale: push your hips into the air. Exhale: lower your toes to the floor.

8

When we give cheerfully and accept gratefully, everyone is blessed.

Maya Angelou

9 Open your arms to the universe and give thanks to Mother Nature.

At any time during your practice, slightly soften and bend your knees to avoid overstraining the muscles on the back of your legs or knees. Yoga is about working with what feels comfortable for you, so move away from discomfort and pain when you feel it.

For every minute you are angry you lose sixty seconds of happiness.

Ralph Waldo Emerson

12 Try the mantra *lam* (pronounced 'l-a-au-m') during meditation as an alternative sound to *om*. Sounds are linked to the main *chakras* to stimulate energy movement. *Lam* is associated with the root *chakra* and the colour red.

13 Break poor sitting habits. Unravel crossed legs when you are sitting on a chair to avoid extra pressure on your hips. Instead, place your feet on the floor to align your hips and provide good support for the rest of your body.

14 Close your eyes, what can you hear? Meditate on the sounds of summer around you and breathe the sweet summer air.

15 To build stamina in your abdominal muscles lie on your back and, as you inhale, lift your legs slightly off the floor. Hold and breathe for as long as you feel comfortable. Lower your legs on an exhalation.

 16 If any good intention has lapsed, recognise this and reset your intentions. Start afresh without guilt or judgement.

Mint has a wonderful aroma and many healing qualities. It is in abundance this time of the year. Infused in hot water, fresh mint makes a refreshing drink to cleanse your digestive system.

 Ignite personal energy in Energy Ball. From a cross-legged position, inhale to prepare yourself. Exhale: bring your knees to your chest and wrap your arms tightly around them. Lower your nose to your knees. Keep still and as small as you can whilst you continue to breathe.

Balance in Standing Extended Leg to build focus and willpower. Begin in Mountain. Inhale: lift your left knee and hold your toes. Exhale: straighten your leg in front of you whilst still holding your toes.

 Honour the longest daylight hours of the year with mindful practice of sun salutation at sunrise and sunset. Give thanks to the circle of life.

 Chop your food finely when you are preparing lunch or dinner to make it easier to chew and for nutrients to be absorbed by digestive juices.

22

The way to do is to be.

Lao Tzu

 23 Be still in Table Top to strengthen your back while stimulating your internal organs. From a Standing Forward Bend, inhale and lift your torso parallel to the earth, rest your palms on your shins or thighs. Hold. Release the position as you exhale.

Combine hula-hooping with yoga breathing to get your energy flowing and your hips moving. Your muscles will be massaged and toned with the circular movement of the hoop, and you will have fun, too!

Sometimes our light goes out, but is blown again into instant flame by an encounter with another human being.

Albert Schweitzer

26 Stand in Tree to cultivate focus and balance. Inhale: place the sole of your left foot on the inside of your right leg (avoiding your knee). Exhale: bring your hands together in Prayer. Repeat on the other side. Hold for as long as you feel balanced and comfortable.

27 Before you leap out of bed in the morning, wake your spine gently to avoid straining your lower back. Lying on your back, inhale and bend your knees to your chest. Rotate your ankles in both directions.

Cut thin slices of cucumber to make soothing, natural eye pads to help reduce puffiness around your eyes.

 Slowly turn your head to release tension in your neck. Inhale. Exhale and gently turn your head to the left. Inhale and turn your head back to the centre. Exhale and repeat to the right. Inhale and return to centre.

 Go green for the day. Drink green-based juices, like spinach or kale. Eat green salad with broccoli to boost your system and fill it with natural goodness.

JULY

1 Run cold water over your wrists to cool your body temperature on a hot summer day. Let the water flow over your pulse points and notice the difference in how you feel.

2 In *Pada bandha*, visualise a triangle of anchor points on the soles of your feet. Focus on your heel, the ball of your big toe and of your little toe. This will create a firm foundation, or rooting, for your feet.

3 Make a natural scrub to exfoliate your face. Mix a teaspoon of brown granulated sugar with three teaspoons of olive oil. Gently rub the mixture into your skin using small circular movements. Rinse with warm water and pat dry.

 4 Walk barefoot in the park, bringing your attention to the sensations of the grass under your feet. Connect with the earth.

 5 Look out for a summer event in your local community and show your support by getting involved.

Apply moisturising cream to your body to rehydrate your skin after exposure to the sun. Use upward strokes towards your heart to help stimulate the lymphatic circulation.

 Acknowledge a new moon during the month as a manifestation of a new cycle to empower the beginning of your own cycle of change.

 Wasps eat bugs and bees pollinate the flowers; both are a positive sight in summer, however both sting to defend themselves. Apply lemon juice directly on a fresh sting to neutralise the alkaline within it.

Drink plenty of water to help flush out toxins after your practice.

 Stand in Dance of Shiva to improve your balance. Start in Mountain. Inhale: lift your left knee so your upper leg is parallel to the floor. Exhale: bend your right elbow 90 degrees in front of you, left arm behind.

 Aim to eat a colourful plate of food every day to guarantee a variety of the minerals and antioxidants that are essential for a healthy body.

Renew energy in your shoulders, especially after heavy physical work, with this standing pose. Inhale: squeeze your shoulder blades together. Feel your muscles compress. Exhale: roll your shoulders forwards. Feel the warm rush of blood to this area.

The best way to find yourself is to lose yourself in the service of others.

Mahatma Gandhi

14

The unselfish effort to bring cheer to others will be the beginning of a happier life for ourselves.

Helen Keller

15 To make a refreshing lemonade, place three roughly chopped unwaxed lemons, 50 g sugar (2–3 tbsp honey) and 500 ml water into a blender. Blitz and then press the mixture through a sieve. Dilute with water to taste, and then chill.

16 Practise yoga with a friend; support each other to make adjustments and suggestions to help refine your postures.

17 Watch butterflies fluttering about their daily business on a hot summer's day. Bring qualities of their movement, lightness, grace and agility into your movements during your practice.

18 When the moment feels right for you, concentrate on your exhalation in *Charlie's Angels Mudra* to direct spent energy away from your body. Place your index fingers together. Interlock your remaining fingers, cross your thumbs and point your index fingers so stale energy shoots away from your body.

Shelter from the heat of the sun under the shade of a tree to keep cool. Give thanks to the tree for its protection.

 Stretch your waist in Standing Crescent to give additional tone and strength to your stomach muscles. Inhale: bring your palms together above your head. Exhale: bend to the left. Remember to stretch the right side. Repeat as many times as you like.

 Release tension in your lower back in a One-Legged Standing Balance. Standing straight in Mountain. Inhale: lift your left knee. Exhale: wrap your hands around it and bend your elbows to bring your knee closer to your chest. Repeat on the other side.

To tone your stomach and to build stamina in your abdominal muscles, lie on your back. As you inhale, lift your legs slightly off the floor. Engage your stomach muscles and buttocks to stabilise your back. Hold and breathe, and then lower your legs on an exhalation.

 Why not place a damp folded cloth over your eyes when you relax in Corpse? The extra dark, cool environment is a perfect way to rest tired eyes.

 Be open to saying 'yes' today. Embrace new opportunities that come your way, actively accept an invitation, an offer of help or an act of kindness.

25 Take advantage of a clear night sky bejewelled with twinkling stars. Spend some time stargazing and look out for shooting stars.

 26 Remember to remove your watch while you practise. It is time to breathe and be in the moment. No need to clock watch!

27

Blessed are the flexible, for they shall not be bent out of shape.

Anonymous

The blossom of meditation
is an expressible peace
that permeates the
entire being. Its fruit…
is indescribable.

Swami Vishnu-Devananda

 29 Try drinking fresh coconut water to replenish your body, especially after practice. It is a rich source of electrolytes, which are responsible for keeping the body properly hydrated so the muscles and nerves can function properly.

30 To strengthen your buttocks and thighs try Chair. Stand in Mountain. Inhale. Exhale, and with knees, ankles and heels together, bend your knees lowering yourself onto an imaginary chair. Bring your hands into Prayer position.

31 Wrap a thoughtful gift for someone and give it to him or her with a 'happy present day' message. Enjoy the pleasure of giving.

AUGUST

⭐**1** To soothe sinuses irritated by a high pollen count, cover your head with a towel and bring your face over a bowl of hot water. Breathe deeply for ten minutes.

⭐**2** Tune in to the gentle noise of summer leaves rustling in the trees. Actively feel the breeze cooling your skin and enjoy the sensation.

⭐**3** Move slowly in the heat, and wear a sun hat, sunglasses and sun cream to protect yourself from the power of the sun.

AUGUST

4 Refresh your energy flow by taking regular breaks throughout the day. Inhale: bring your hands above your head and interlock your fingers. Exhale: turn your palms towards the sky. Hold and breathe deeply.

5 Freeze fresh, natural juice to make nutritious home-made ice lollies to cool you down on a hot day.

6 Your mind and your body are intrinsically linked. If muscles are relaxed, your mind is relaxed; if your mind is tense, your body is stressed. Inhale for a count of four and exhale for a count of eight to harmonise both.

AUGUST

 Allow your thoughts to pass through your mind like clouds on a summer day. Breathe into this calm image while you meditate today to keep your mind free of distraction.

 Sound the mantra *vam* (pronounced 'v-a-au-m'), associated to the sacral *chakra*, during your meditation to release energy in the base of your spine to ground yourself and to feel personal connection with your mind, body and spirit.

 In stressful moments we unwittingly tighten our buttocks. Mindfully relax your buttock muscles and pummel them with your fists to release stored emotional energy.

Most folks are usually
about as happy as they
make their minds up to be.

Abraham Lincoln

 Your lungs are like balloons – inflating,
deflating, driven by muscular action of
the diaphragm. Each lung is about the
size of a football. Visualise your lungs
filling to full capacity to maximise
breathing potential.

A photographer gets people to pose for him. A yoga instructor gets people to pose for themselves.

Terri Guillemets

 Try a new style of yoga. There are many styles to explore: Sivanada, Iyengar, Kundalini, Ashtanga, Hot/Bikram, Partner, Yin and Laughter yoga. Which suits you?

 Be creative: invent your own *asana* to personalise your practice.

Buy a selection of potted fresh herbs to give you a choice of fragrant flavourings to use in cooking. Repot the herbs to encourage growth.

 Celebrate summer. Enjoy eating outside to boost your mood and to absorb energy from the sun. Contact with the sun on your skin produces essential vitamin D, which is good for your heart and immune system.

 Go foraging for blackberries in your local area. Use them in a fresh fruit salad or freeze them for winter.

Stand in a Wide-Legged Forward Bend, toes slightly turned inwards, to help unblock a stuffy head. Inhale: circle your arms above your head. Exhale: fold forwards with your legs straight. Let your arms and head hang loosely. Breathe. Remember to work with how you feel, slightly bend your knees if you feel any strain.

 Practise Locust to strengthen your buttocks, legs, arms and shoulders. Lie on your front. Inhale: extend your arms forwards, palms facing down. Exhale. Inhale: lift your legs and arms. Exhale: lower legs and arms.

Bring the positive virtues of honesty, kindness, compassion, love, understanding and patience into your day to be the best person you can be.

 Butterfly your knees in Happy Seat to open your hips. Move your knees up and down quickly like a butterfly's wings to encourage energy flow to this area.

 Eat water-rich natural foods such as watermelon, celery, cucumber, lettuce and tomatoes to help hydrate your body.

Avocado is a superfood, packed with healthy fats and high levels of vitamins that are good for your heart. You can also mash the flesh and use it as a face mask. Smear a thin layer directly onto your skin and leave for five to ten minutes to let the goodness be absorbed. Rinse with water and pat dry.

Happiness is when what you think, what you say and what you do are in harmony.

Mahatma Gandhi

25

I will not be distracted by noise, chatter or setbacks. Patience, commitment, grace and purpose will guide me.

Louise Hay

26 As tempting as it is, refrain from scratching irritated skin. Soothe itchy skin with cold water, and focus on your breath, rather than the itch, to reduce the prickly sensation.

AUGUST

 27 Develop focus, balance and upper body strength in Crane. Place your hands on the floor shoulder distance apart. Bend your knees and rest them on the back of your upper arms. Inhale. Exhale and lift your feet. Refrain if your wrists are feeling weak.

 28 When resting or sleeping on your side, place a cushion or pillow between your legs to separate your knees and help keep your hips aligned.

 29 Use *Agni Mudra* to improve digestion during your meditation. Connect your thumb and middle finger on each hand, and extend the first, third and fourth fingers away from the palm. Breathe.

AUGUST

 Sway your arms from side to side, twisting at your waist and keeping your hips facing forward, to loosen your spine after sitting still on a long journey.

 Take responsibility for your well-being by monitoring your toilet movements to check your state of health. Dark urine could indicate that your kidneys are working under pressure to remove toxins. Drink water to rebalance your system.

SEPTEMBER

1 Concentrate on Backbends in your evening practice to elevate your mood. Keep your chest and heart lifted as you breathe all the way down into the small of your back.

2 Focus on micro-adjustments available to you during your practice. On your inhalation feel your body expand, swelling with new energy; as you exhale, gently move into the spaces you create in your body.

Back to school for children, students and teachers; why not join them? Enrol for an evening class. It is never too late to learn.

 Embrace the lightness and joy that yoga ignites. Feel free to smile through your practice and shine!

 Prepare your food with your full attention and always let love be a main ingredient.

SEPTEMBER

 Organise a fun social gathering to nurture new friendships with fellow yogis in your class.

 Notice a detail in nature: the spiral of a snail's shell, the pattern in the veins of a leaf or the delicacy in a petal. Remind yourself you are part of nature.

 Stand in Eagle to deepen your balance. Start in Mountain. Inhale: wrap your left leg around your standing right leg. Exhale. Inhale: twist your arms together in front of your body, joining your palms. Exhale: slightly bend your knees. Repeat on the other side.

9 Have a quiet day to yourself: switch off your phone and avoid the computer and the television. Find solace in your own silence and inner peace.

10 Sit in a Tail Bone Balance to focus your mind. Begin in Staff. Bring your knees to your chest. Wrap your arms around them. Inhale and lift your feet off the floor, finding balance on your tail bone. Hold and breathe.

11 Yoga is beneficial to everyone, of every size, shape and age. Be gentle with yourself, know your limits and avoid comparing yourself to others.

Whatever you do to one side of your body in yoga, repeat the same movement on the other side to keep left and right balanced.

To think creatively, we must be able to look afresh at what we normally take for granted.

George Keller

14

Ultimately spiritual awareness unfolds when you're flexible... when you're detached, when you're easy on yourself and easy on others.

Deepak Chopra

15 When gases are released from the fluid surrounding your joints, they can create an audible popping sound. This is a natural process, although forcing your joints to crack is unnatural.

16 Pay attention to the abundance of colour in nature as the leaves turn yellow, orange and red, ready to fall. Consider how these changes are part of the cycle of the natural year.

17 Re-energise aching shoulders with simple shoulder lifts. Inhale: lift your shoulders towards your ears. Exhale: push them down. Repeat several times with slow, mindful breath.

18 Every day is an opportunity to create change in your life.

Embrace the intensity of colours in the sky at sunset as autumn settles in.

 Try Thread the Needle to relax your shoulders. Begin in Child pose. Inhale: extend your left arm under and across your body. Exhale. Inhale: raise your right arm skyward and as you exhale slowly lower it to join both hands together.

 Nerve endings in your hands send messages throughout your body, communicating with your nervous system. Clap your hands together to stimulate your nervous system.

SEPTEMBER

 22 Your wrists are made up of eight individual bones, making them delicate parts of your body. To ease the pressure of aching wrists, use your knuckles or fingertips in your practice instead of pressing flat palms onto the floor.

 23 Look out for the early evening harvest moon. It is the first full moon closest to the autumn equinox.

 24 Combine a balance with a hand stretch to open your heart. Start in Tree. Inhale and bring your arms above your head. As you exhale, stretch your fingers wide, palms facing forwards. Hold and breathe as you balance for as long as you can.

Yoga is your personal 'tool box' to dip in to and to utilise whenever needed. Make your practice work for you.

You only live once, but if you do it right, once is enough.

Mae West

There are only two
ways to live your life.
One is as though
nothing is a miracle.
The other is as though
everything is a miracle.

Albert Einstein

 Be patient with yourself, switch off
the critical, negative voice and promote
positive thoughts. Negativity eats away
at you; positivity serves you.

SEPTEMBER

 29 Deepen your stomach breathing in Corpse. Lightly place your hands on your stomach. Inhale and feel your hands rise as your stomach rises. Leave your hands where they are and notice your navel sink towards your spine as you exhale.

 30 Starting in a kneeling position, breathe deeply in Cow Face to increase flexibility in your upper body. Inhale: stretch your hands above your head. Exhale: circle your left hand behind and up between your shoulder blades. Bend your right arm over your right shoulder, aiming to join your hands together. Flexibility will come with time and patience.

OCTOBER

 In the West we sit on chairs, causing stiffness and inflexibility in the hips. Bring yourself down to the floor and sit in cross-legged position instead of sitting on the settee. Notice how upright and relaxed you feel in this position.

 When you are landing or jumping back from a position, think the words 'land lightly', so that you move consciously and mindfully.

In the same way that you make space in your body and mind, also try to free up other areas of your life. Clean up your smartphone for instance, by deleting unnecessary numbers and unwanted emails in your inbox.

 Balance in Boat to clear your mind. Begin in Energy Ball. Inhale. Exhale and extend your legs, keeping balance on your tail bone. Extend your arms in front of you or bring them above your head to deepen the pose.

As soon as you get home, remove your shoes and socks. Move, stretch and flex your toes to liberate them after being restricted in shoes all day.

 Drink ginger tea to boost your immunsystem to protect against colds, coughs and splutters. Add thin slices of fresh ginger to a cup of hot water.

 Visualise the power and strength of ocean waves as they rhythmically roll in and out of the shore to help deepen your breathing pattern.

8 When did you last replace your bed linen, pillows, toothbrush, towels, underwear or socks? Replace any you have had for a long time; old towels in particular can develop a pungent smell.

9

Feelings come and go like clouds in a windy sky. Conscious breathing is my anchor.

Thích Nhất Hạnh

10 Wear leg or arm warmers to provide additional warmth and to keep the cold away from your wrists and ankles.

There is no such thing as bad weather, only different kinds of good weather.

John Ruskin

Place an object (for example, a stone or pen) on the end of your finger to explore your sense of balance. Challenge yourself to move around preventing the object from falling off your finger.

 Practise *Yoni Mudra* to bring concentration and calm to your mind. Close your ears with your thumbs, close your eyes with your index fingers and your nostrils with your middle fingers, and press your lips together with the remaining fingers. Observe a sense of tranquillity as you breathe deeply for a few minutes.

Choose the mantra *ram* (pronounced 'r-a-au-m') to stimulate energy flow in your third *chakra*, the navel area. Focus on yellow, the colour associated with this *chakra*.

 Ease stiffness from your neck with a gentle head roll. Inhale to prepare. Exhale: lower your chin to your chest. Inhale: slowly roll your head to the left. Exhale: roll your chin back to chest. Inhale: roll your head to the right. Exhale: return your chin to the chest.

Cup your hands around your knees and begin to rub round and round, in one direction, then the other. This gentle circular movement warms, relaxes and soothes joints. Give your elbows the same treatment!

 No matter how grey the sky looks, the sky is still blue above the clouds.

 Collect some delicious, heart-warming soup recipes to comfort and fuel you through the winter.

19 Go for a sauna or Turkish bath to absorb deep heat into your muscles, bones and joints.

20 Have a complaint-free day! Move through your day without complaining. Promote the positive in every situation and focus less on the negative.

21 Our emotional and physical needs change constantly; pay attention to how you are feeling, and tap into your emotional self throughout the day for personal harmony.

22 Learn to listen to and to follow your instincts.

If you feel exhausted from your day, with little time for your practice before you are on the move again, lie on your back and take a moment in Corpse to regain your equilibrium.

Love and compassion are necessities, not luxuries. Without them, humanity cannot survive.

Dalai Lama

25

If you want to conquer the anxiety of life, live in the moment, live in the breath.

Amit Ray

26 Stretch the entire front of your body in Bow. Lie on your front. Inhale: bend your knees towards your buttocks. Exhale: hold onto your feet. Inhale: lift your chest and knees. Release as you exhale.

Notice the change of the daylight hour as the clocks go back. Burn a candle to celebrate light.

 Blocked up and stuffy with a cold? Blow your nose one nostril at a time to avoid forceful blowing. Blowing your nose hard pushes mucus back into the sinuses.

 The tongue is a muscle without which you cannot speak. In a quiet moment roll, curl, extend, twist and push up and down with your tongue to mindfully exercise it.

30 Efficient circulation depends on a healthy heart. Practise your favourite *asana* to promote positive energy flow. All *asanas* are beneficial to your mind, body and spirit.

 31 Carve a pumpkin and illuminate it with a candle to create a seasonal atmosphere during your practice. Use the flesh to make a savoury dish, a pumpkin dip or a delicious pumpkin pie.

NOVEMBER

1 Hang bags of bird-friendly nuts to help hungry birds with their daily quest for food. Winter is a challenging time for them too!

2 Treat your body to a massage. Comment in your diary on the feelings you experienced and the sensations you noticed before and after your massage.

3 Be curious in the kitchen and get baking to fill your house with the warm smell of freshly baked treats. Share them with your friends.

Be strong and stable in Triangle. Stand in Wide Legged Standing position. Inhale: swivel your left foot sideways, raise your arms to make a 'T' at shoulder height. Exhale: reach to the left, then lower your left hand to the floor. Lift your right arm above your head and turn your head skywards.

 Use *yam* (pronounced 'y-a-au-m'), the mantra meditation connected to the heart *chakra*, to open energy flow in the heart. Surround yourself with the colour green, which is the colour associated with the fourth *chakra*.

Eat fresh pineapple to soothe a sore throat. Pineapple contains bromelain, an enzyme that has anti-inflammatory properties as well as many other vitamins and minerals that will help you on the road to recovery.

 Stimulate your colon, liver and kidneys whilst opening your hips in Baby Cradle. Begin in Staff. Inhale. Exhale: bend and lift your left knee out to the side, cradle your knee and left lower leg in your arms. Gently rock it side to side for as long as you like.

Work on overall body strength to improve your general practice. Breathe in Half Plank, resting on your elbows and forearms instead of on your hands. Hold for as long as you feel comfortable.

 Be still in Hero to relieve high blood pressure. Kneel with your feet hip distance apart. Inhale: circle both arms above your head. Exhale: lower your buttocks to the floor. Rest your palms on your knees.

Without winter no one would appreciate and love summer so much. Visit the tree that gave you shade during the hot summer and give thanks to its continual seasonal growth.

How people treat you is their karma; how you react is yours.

Wayne Dyer

Everyone has a skill or talent to share. Organise a skill swap with someone and share the mutual benefit.

You cannot control the results, only your actions.

Allan Lokos

NOVEMBER

 Trim your fingernails and toenails to keep them clean and germ free to reduce the likelihood of catching infections and colds.

 Twist in Chair to help release stiffness in your back. Start in Chair. Inhale and bring hands to Prayer. Exhale and bring your right elbow to your left knee. Look skywards. Hold. Breathe. Repeat on the other side.

 A significant amount of body temperature is lost through your head. To retain your body warmth, wear a cosy hat or hoodie, especially after a yoga class.

17 Frequently wriggle, waggle, shake and bend your fingers during the day to keep the blood flowing and maintain warmth. They get cold with poor circulation.

18 Rustle up a delicious spicy vegetable curry for dinner. As well as providing wonderful flavour and aroma, garlic will cleanse the blood, turmeric will flush the liver and cumin has anti-carcinogenic properties.

19 Put some fresh lavender under your pillow and have an early night. A good night's sleep helps the body to function.

20 Cloves attack germs and are a natural painkiller. Put a clove under your tongue to help rid a sore throat or soothe a toothache.

 21 Whistle, hum or sing a merry tune to help lift your spirits.

 22 Increase circulation to your kidneys in Side Open Angle. Sit with your legs spread as wide as possible, hips facing forwards. Inhale. Exhale and extend your arms, aiming to hold your left foot. Repeat on the other side.

Energise your lower back in Upward-Facing Dog. Lie on your front. Place your hands on the floor below your shoulders. Inhale and push onto the tops of your toes, lifting your chest and lower body off the ground.

 The normal spine is a gently curved 'S' shape naturally designed to distribute the weight of your bones and keep your body upright. Think, 'I am long, lovely and erect,' to avoid slumping and slouching into your spine.

 Calm your mind and reduce stress and anxiety levels by spending longer in Plough today. Lie on your back. Inhale: bring your legs above your head. Exhale: lower them slowly to the floor behind you. Hold. Breathe.

Be yourself, everyone else is taken.

Oscar Wilde

27

Desire, ask, believe, receive.

Stella Terrill Mann

28 Relax your lower back in a gentle Reclined Twist. Lie on your back. Inhale. Exhale: bend your knees to your chest. Inhale. Exhale: lower your knees to the right, turn your head to the left. Repeat on the other side.

You cannot do yoga.
Yoga is your natural
state. What you can
do are yoga exercises,
which may reveal to you
where you are resisting
your natural state.

Sharon Gannon

 Arrange a play date with friends. How about rollerblading, trampolining or having a spa day? Whatever you do, have fun!

1 A Shoulder Stand is an ideal pick-me-up. Start in Plough. Inhale and slowly bring your legs directly above your head. Support the small of your back with your hands, fingertips pointing skywards. Hold. Breathe.

2 Warm up the tiny muscles in your feet to avoid straining them before slipping into your party shoes. Rotate your ankles, flex and extend your feet. Inhale: lift onto your toes. Exhale: lower down to the floor.

DECEMBER

 3 Contemplate the shape and structure of a naked winter tree to see the similarities between you and a tree: its trunk is your body; its roots your feet; its branches your arms and legs; and its twigs your fingers and toes.

 4 Exercise your jaw to release stress built up from clenching and gritting. Close your eyes. Inhale and slowly open your mouth as wide as you can. Exhale and gently close your mouth. Repeat eight times.

 5 Relax at the end of the day in Frontal Corpse. Lie on your front with your big toes touching. Create a cushion with your hands and lay your head to one side. Breathe.

Visualise yourself surrounded by light to shield your personal energy from the demands of the outside world and the negativity of others.

 Set an affirmation for the day, week or month ahead to make you conscious of positive thought. Create a short powerful statement and assert that what you want to be true, is true.

 Choose the mantra *ham* (pronounced 'h-a-au-m') during meditation to focus your attention on your throat *chakra* to free your voice. Wear blue, which is the colour associated with the fifth *chakra*.

Have fun on a snowy day and let your inner child be free. Go sledging, make a snow sculpture, crunch through the snow or make snow angels in your own image.

Have only love in your heart for others. The more you see the good in them, the more you will establish good in yourself.

Paramahansa Yogananda

11

We are what our thoughts have made us; so take care about what you think. Words are secondary. Thoughts live; they travel far.

Swami Vivekananda

12 Bone-building activity is stimulated by carrying and lifting weight. See your extra bags of shopping as a productive workout, rather than a chore.

Considered to be the king of *asanas*, a Headstand requires concentration and the body strength to protect the spine. Practise against a wall to build confidence and seek guidance from your teacher to avoid injury.

 Energise your mind in Wheel. Lie on your back. Inhale: bend your knees, placing your feet on the floor as close to your buttocks as possible. Bring your hands under your shoulders, fingers pointing towards your feet. Inhale: lift your body. Hold. Breathe. Lower on an exhalation.

15 Drink hot camomile tea to soothe a cold. Dampen cotton wool pads with cold camomile tea to ease sore eyes if they are inflamed from a lot of sneezing.

 16 Keep your levels of vitamin C topped up by eating plenty of fruit to protect you from winter colds and germs.

 17 Unwind in a deep hot bath to relax your muscles, reduce cramps and relieve tension headaches. Similar to the effect of a massage, a good hot soak will relax your muscles.

DECEMBER

 Take a seated meditation using *Abhaya Mudra*, the hand gesture of fearlessness. Raise your right hand to chest level with your palm facing forward. Extend your fingers skywards with the intention of bringing emotional energy and courage into your heart.

 Release energy flow in your spine in Knee to Ear. Start in Plough. Inhale. Exhale: bend your knees to your ears. Extend your arms against the floor in the opposite direction to your feet, palms facing down.

Tap into your core strength in Lateral Plank. From Plank, inhale and turn on your toes bringing the outer edge of your right foot to connect with the floor. Lift your left arm skywards. Hold. Breathe. Repeat on the other side.

 Lighten up the shortest day of the year with candles and fairy lights. Remind yourself that daylight hours will be a fraction longer tomorrow!

 To reduce general fatigue in your legs, ankles and feet, lie on your back, with a cushion or rolled blanket underneath your knees. Relax with your arms away from your body, palms facing up. Breathe.

DECEMBER

 Lie on your back with bent knees to shift a bloated feeling. Inhale. Exhale: bend and wrap your arms around your knees. Slowly squeeze them to your chest. Gently rock forwards and backwards on your spine to expel any trapped wind.

 Tension causes muscle fibres to tighten, restricting blood flow and leading to the development of sore areas known as 'knots'. Relax on your back for five minutes or longer with a tennis ball under the knot to help break down the tenderness.

 A hug is not just for Christmas! It is one of the nicest presents you can give all year round.

The body makes between one to two litres of saliva daily, less while sleeping. Chewing helps to stimulate saliva production within the mouth. Chew your food thoroughly to help the manufacture of this essential digestive juice.

 Treat yourself to new comfortable clothing for yoga, or a new yoga mat for the year ahead.

 Be the designer of your own life; create dreams and then make them come true. Live your life!

Look back through your diary to see the changes you have experienced and the positive steps you have made throughout the year. However small or large your steps have been, they all help to create a better you!

 Take strength from endings as they create space for new beginnings.

 Namaste – the divine light in me recognises the divine light in you.